Piano • Vocal • Guitar

RODRIGUEZ

SELECTIONS FROM COLD FACT & COMING FROM REALITY

ISBN 978-1-4803-6102-7

HAL•LEONARD®
CORPORATION

7777 W. BLUEMOUND RD. P.O. BOX 13819 MILWAUKEE, WI 53213

Visit Hal Leonard Online at
www.halleonard.com

CAN'T GET AWAY

Words and Music by
SIXTO DIAZ RODRIGUEZ

Born in the trou-bled cit-y in
Schooled on the cit-y side-walks,
Go-ing un-aid-ed to the West Coast,

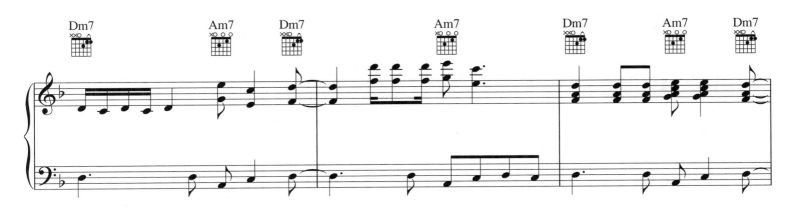

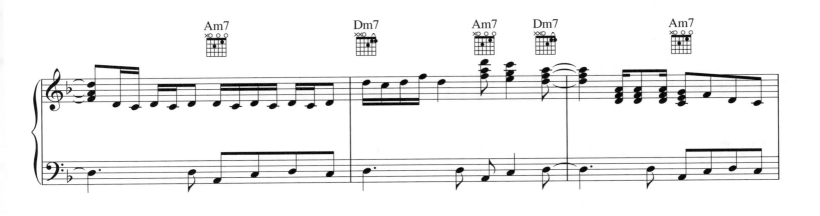

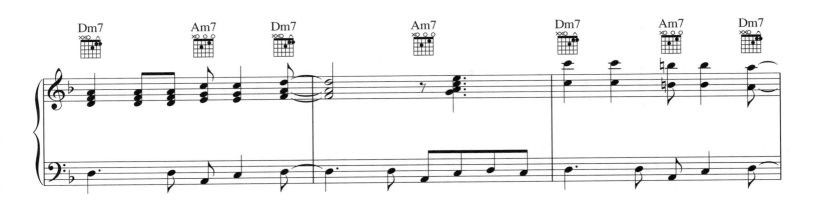

D.S. al Coda

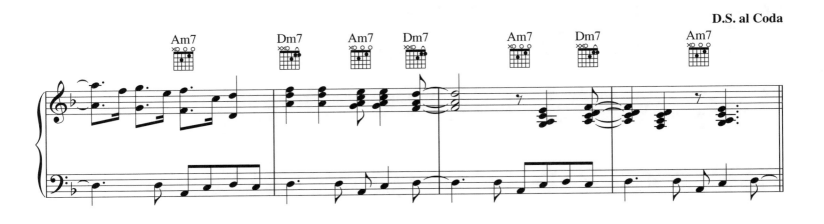

CAUSE

Words and Music by
SIXTO DIAZ RODRIGUEZ

Folk Ballad

Additional Lyrics

2. 'Cause my heart's become a crooked hotel full of rumors,
   But it's I who pays the rent for these fingered-face out-of-tuners.
   And I make sixteen solid half-hour friendships every evening,
   'Cause your Queen of Hearts who's half a stone and likes to laugh alone
   Is always threatening you with leaving.
   Oh, but they'll play those token games on Willy Thompson
   And give a medal to replace the son of Mrs. Annie Johnson.

3. 'Cause they told me everybody's got to pay their dues,
   And I explained that I had overpaid them.
   So overdued I went to the company store,
   And the clerk there said that they had just been invaded.
   So I set sail in a teardrop and escaped beneath the doorsill,
   'Cause the smell of her perfume echoes in my head still.

CLIMB UP ON MY MUSIC

Words and Music by
SIXTO DIAZ RODRIGUEZ

Funk Rock

Have you ev - er _____ had a fe - ver
_____ girl named Christ - mas.
_____ been in dark - ness

from a bit - ter - sweet re - frain? _____
Did I tell you _____ she drank gold? _____
and your mind could _____ she find no peace _____

Have you ev - er _____ kissed the sun - shine,
She was - n't ver - y hard to cap - ture,
when you woke up _____ af - ter mid - night,

Well, there was a ___ ___

Guitar solo - ad lib.

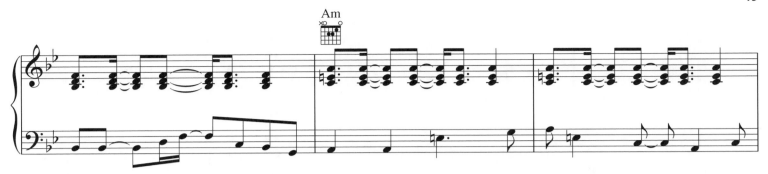

D.S. al Coda

Solo ends

Have you ev-er __

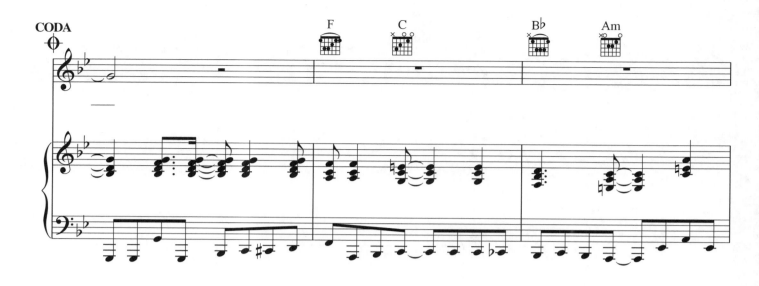

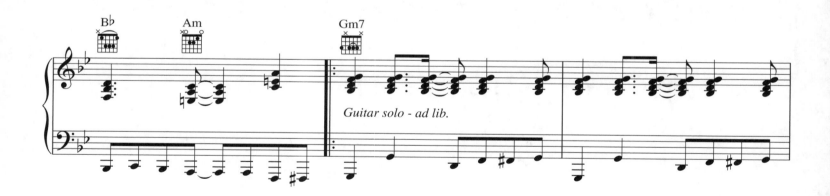

Guitar solo - ad lib.

Repeat and Fade | **Optional Ending**

CRUCIFY YOUR MIND

Words and Music by
SIXTO DIAZ RODRIGUEZ

Was it a hunts-man or ___ a play-er ___ that
Soon, you know, ___ I'll leave you ___ and I'll

made you pay the cost ___ that now as-sumes re-laxed ___ po-si-tions ___ and
nev-er look be-hind, ___ 'cause I was born ___ for ___ the pur-pose ___ that

I THINK OF YOU

Words and Music by
SIXTO DIAZ RODRIGUEZ

And ___ think ___ of you, ___

and I do. ___

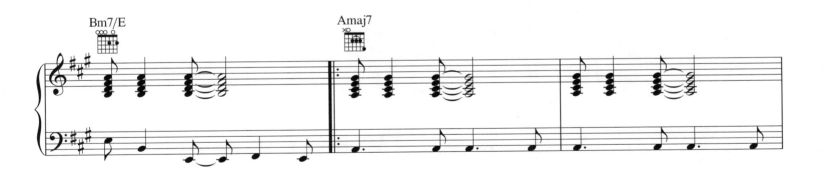

Repeat and Fade | **Optional Ending**

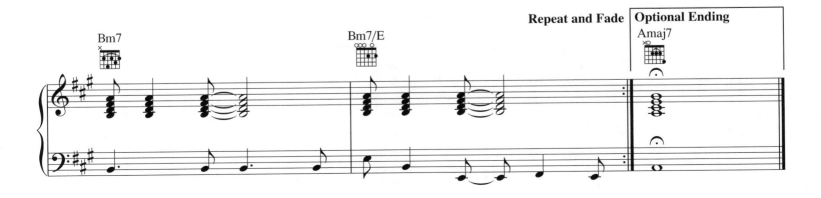

I WONDER

Words and Music by
SIXTO DIAZ RODRIGUEZ

(1., 4.) won - der   how man - y times ___ you've been had ___ and   I
(2.) won - der   a - bout the love ___ you can't find ___ and   I I
(3.) won - der   a - bout the tears in chil - dren's eyes ___ and   I

* 4th time: dreams

won - der, I do. ____
won - der, I do. ____
won - der; don't you? ____

1–3

2. I
3. I
4. I

4

INNER CITY BLUES

Words and Music by
SIXTO DIAZ RODRIGUEZ

Go - ing down a dirt - y in - ner - cit - y side road, I plot - ted.

Recorded a half step lower.

34

CODA

Go-ing down a dust-y Geor-gi - an-a side _ road, I won - der.

The wind splashed _ in my face, can smell a trace of thun-

- der.

Repeat and Fade | Optional Ending

I'LL SLIP AWAY

Words and Music by
SIXTO RODRIGUEZ

* Recorded a half step lower.

JANE S. PIDDY

Words and Music by
SIXTO DIAZ RODRIGUEZ

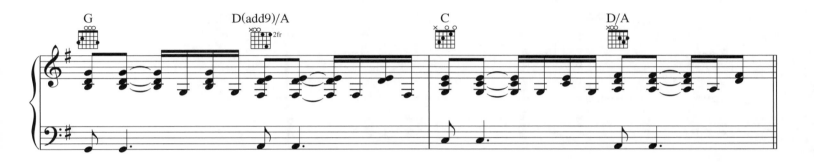

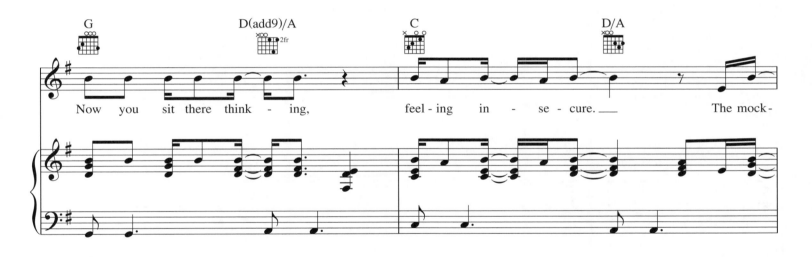

Now you sit there think-ing, feel-ing in - se - cure.___ The mock-

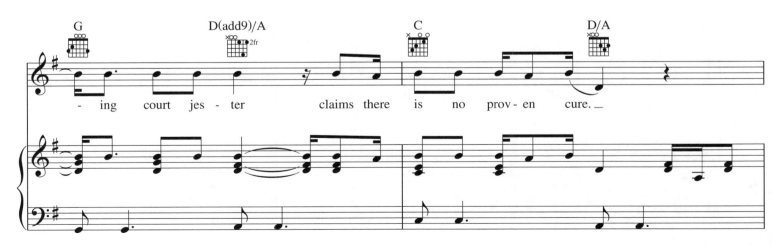

-ing court jes - ter claims there is no prov - en cure.___

LIKE JANIS

Words and Music by
SIXTO DIAZ RODRIGUEZ

Bright Folk Rock

And you meas - ure for wealth ___ by the things ___ you can hold. ___
And you want to be held ___ with high - est re - gard. ___

___ And you meas - ure for love ___ by the sweet ___ things you're told. ___
It de - lights you so much ___ if he's try - ing so hard. ___

D.S. al Coda

meas - ure it dead. _____

'Cause _

CODA

_____

and sit there in won - der and doubt _

for me? ___

Repeat and Fade | **Optional Ending**

STREET BOY

Words and Music by
SIXTO DIAZ RODRIGUEZ

Street ___ boy, ___ you've been out ___

___ too ___ long. ___ Street ___ boy, ___ ain't you got e - nough

SUGAR MAN

Words and Music by
SIXTO DIAZ RODRIGUEZ

Moderate Folk Rock

Sug - ar Man, _____ won't _____ you
_____ met _____ a
_____ you're _____ the

hur - ry?   'Cause I'm _____ ti - red of _____ these scenes. _____   For a blue
false friend   on a _____ lone - ly, dust - y road. _____   Lost my heart;
an - swer   that makes _____ my ques - tions dis - ap - pear. _____   Sug - ar Man,

THIS IS NOT A SONG, IT'S AN OUTBURST

Words and Music by
SIXTO DIAZ RODRIGUEZ